Hardwick Old Hall

Susie West

Introduction

Hardwick Old Hall was built between 1587 and 1596 by Bess of Hardwick, one of the richest and best-connected women of the Elizabethan age. It was a radical modern mansion, drawing on the latest Italian innovations in house design.

Bess of Hardwick is almost as famous for her four marriages as she is for her building activities. She was married at 15, but her young husband, Robert Barlow, died a year later. She outlived three more husbands, all Elizabethan courtiers, bore eight children and became an intimate friend of the queen. After the violent collapse of her fourth marriage to the earl of Shrewsbury, Bess retreated to her family estate at Hardwick.

As a countess, Bess needed something grander than her father's medieval manor house. She began to build Hardwick Old Hall in its place in 1587, making use of its bold views across the open Derbyshire landscape. In 1590, Bess began building another house immediately adjacent – the New Hall – this time using a professional architect, Robert Smythson. The Old and New Halls were intended to complement each other, like two wings of one building.

Bess died in 1608, leaving her son, William Cavendish, in charge of Hardwick. William was the founder of the Cavendish family, dukes of Devonshire, still based at the Chatsworth estate that Bess and his father purchased. The dukes came to prefer Chatsworth, and partially dismantled the Old Hall in the 1750s.

Above: Detail from a portrait of Bess as a young woman

Facing page: The two halls built by Bess sit proudly in their Elizabethan garden setting

Tour

Hardwick Old Hall was the family home of Bess of Hardwick. Bess completely remodelled the old manor house in the 1580s and 1590s to produce a much grander house, better suited to the needs of a countess. Much of the house was dismantled by the 1750s, and it is only possible to see some of the upper rooms from ground level.

FOLLOWING THE TOUR
The tour starts in the courtyard, from where it is possible to see the main rooms in the house. Visitors are then directed to the kitchen and services and then upstairs, to get a better view of some of the upper rooms.

THE HOUSE

The house was built of local sandstone between 1587 and 1596. It was finished with rough plaster, a little of which still clings to the south wall. It was slightly extended by additional lodgings in the north-east tower, added in 1608.

The courtyard of the Old Hall is protected by a high stone wall and the two corner lodges. The entrance gateway is a simple classical door frame, very similar to the fragments of the Old Hall porch doorway across the courtyard. To the left and right are lodges, built in about 1625. They have two rooms on each floor with a central staircase. Each room has a spacious window and a fireplace, so they were probably intended as extra accommodation for higher status servants or for those of a visiting household. The west lodge rear exit leads into the service court, now empty of most of the stores, and back out into the north forecourt. The service court was partially enclosed by a tennis court, here by 1642 and possibly connected to a visit by Prince Charles (the future Charles I) in 1619.

THE SETTING

The two great houses, along with the surrounding parkland, boundary walls and stable court, survive today in the same relationship that Bess knew from the 1590s. After her death in 1608, a survey map of the property was drawn up, recording its essential components (see page 32). In Bess's day, however, the approach to the property was rather more dramatic than today. Elizabethan visitors would have kept to the lower ground beneath the back of the house, before making a sudden climb

Facing page: Detail of the south front of the Old Hall, showing the stair turret and main gable over the great hall range

Below: A cutaway reconstruction drawing of the Old Hall
1 Forest Great Chamber
2 Hill Great Chamber
3 Roof walks
4 Best Bedchamber suite
5 Great Hall
6 Kitchen and services
7 Lodges

to arrive through the gateway in the centre of the outer grass court.

The stone for the hall was quarried from the park, in the lower ground to the south. The quarry is still visible from the exit road. Timber was a valuable resource that could have come from the Hardwick estate. Bess also owned profitable glass workshops, and she mined lead from the Peak District, so her wider estates supported the construction of both the halls here.

■ GREAT HALL AND ■ GREAT STAIRS

The novel, symmetrical layout of Hardwick owes much to Italian Renaissance villas. Bess placed the great hall in the centre of the house, with the front door in the centre of the short end wall (see plan on inside back cover). This went against the medieval tradition of placing the door asymmetrically at one end of the hall.

The entrance to the house is, however, now something of a puzzle, as the porch was completely rebuilt after the demolition of this half of the building, and it might not have been correctly reconstructed. There are also two plaques, dated 1904, set into the back of the porch. The central door into the hall has been blocked and the lower lights of the surviving window have also been filled in, and it is not clear when or why this was done.

The surviving details in the great hall suggest that it was fairly plain, compared with the rest of the interiors. It was double-height with plaster walls, well lit by four tall windows. The heraldic overmantel would have taken pride of place; it is one of many visible around the house. The stag is the symbol of the Cavendish family, as Sir William Cavendish was Bess's second husband and the father of her eight children. The central panel has been cut out, and was probably a heraldic shield.

Above: The remains of the fireplace and heraldic overmantel in the great hall

Below: A reconstruction drawing of the hall, using the evidence from the inventory made in 1601. The hall was simply furnished

Daily Life at Hardwick

Bess had a very important social position to maintain, not just because of her wealth. At the time, people believed that the maintenance of society depended on the proper observance of ritual and etiquette. Aristocrats maintained their own versions of a royal court, with officials from local landowning families employed to run the household and manage their estates. Bess herself finished her education in another aristocratic household by performing minor domestic duties suited to her lesser status. Aristocratic houses, therefore, had to be designed to accommodate many more people than the immediate family and domestic servants. The Old and New Halls would have contained an extended household of gentlemen and gentlewomen. Bess was at the centre of her own court, sitting on the best chair in each room, with matching footstool and cushion; in the Forest Great Chamber, Bess's chair was upholstered with cloth of gold and trimmed with gold and silver fringing.

At all times, Bess was on show to her own household, maintaining her dignity and authority over her adult children and her gentleman officers. As a countess, she had no equal in the region. While she could choose to eat privately (she had a small dining room in each house), she also had to lead her household in going to her private chapel, meeting with her legal and property advisers, overseeing her granddaughter's education, and being available for requests from local aristocratic and gentry families. Of course this also meant she kept up with local gossip, and business opportunities in the region. She made many advantageous purchases of land for her growing estate this way. Daily life for Bess was played out in public, as she was the source of local employment, justice and patronage. She was in her sixties when she began building Hardwick, and still full of energy.

> Bess was at the centre of her own court, sitting on the best chair in each room, with matching footstool and cushion

Above: Detail from a portrait of Sir Henry Unton, showing him at a banquet, while a masque of Mercury and Diana is performed, accompanied by musicians. It was painted in about 1596, when Bess was finishing the Old Hall; she would have hosted similar entertainments

The great hall was where the lower servants and those of visitors took their meals. By the 1580s, aristocratic owners did not generally eat with their servants. Important members of the family and guests lived away from the hall. However, the great hall retained its symbolic importance as the 'heart of the house', where good management and generous hospitality could be seen to be taking place. It was still the first reception room for all visitors, who would have been met by the Elizabethan equivalent of the butler, called the usher. His room was just to the left of the hall. The hall also marks the division between the service areas of the house to the right (west) and the route up the great stairs to the grandest rooms.

The only trace of the doorway to the stairs is a partial jamb in the fireplace wall; and all that is left of the great stairs is a stone base of eroded steps. Only the ghosts of the treads can be seen climbing their way up to the attic. The stair block was a second thought by Bess, inserted later into the corner formed between the great hall and the east range.

At Hardwick, the higher up the stairs, the better the rooms were. The apparent inconvenience of a long walk up to a banquet on the top floor was ignored because the social benefits of being admitted to Bess's world were immense.

Below: *View of the eastern half of the Old Hall, dismantled by the 1750s, showing the Forest Great Chamber's great east window and surviving plaster frieze*

1 Door from great hall
2 Great stairs
3 Forest Great Chamber

⬛ FOREST GREAT CHAMBER

Elizabethan great chambers were important reception rooms, which could be set up for dining, dancing or receiving guests in high state. The Forest Great Chamber takes its name from the deep plaster frieze of trees that fills the upper part of the walls in this third-floor room. Looking up from the basement, it is difficult to tell that the plaster humans modelled in the frieze are roughly life-sized. This double-height room was one of the most lavish interiors in the house. It was so important to Bess that she rebuilt this end of the house to support the weight of this vast reception room. The evidence for this is visible in the south wall, with the curious double supporting walls of the bay windows.

Hardwick Old Hall is very unusual in having two great chambers: this one and the Hill Great Chamber at the west end of the house. In between them was the more intimate, but even more richly furnished, state bedchamber with its withdrawing room and closet. The Forest Great Chamber is at the top of the great stairs and signals the start of a processional route across this floor, culminating in the grandeur of the Hill Great Chamber.

The distinctive decorative plasterwork is also unusual, probably inspired by a now-lost room in Lord Burghley's house at Theobalds, Hertfordshire. Bess's son, Charles, described the room in a letter to her after he visited it in 1587. Theobalds's great chamber had a similar plaster frieze, said to be so realistic that birds nested in it – an elegant compliment for the visual tricks that the Elizabethans enjoyed. Bess hung the walls below the frieze with gilded and painted leather hangings. The only other room in the house to have been decorated in this lavish way was Bess's bedchamber, which had seven lengths of painted and gilded leather. From the household accounts, we know that she had 85 lengths stored in the attic, representing a costly investment in craftsmanship, perhaps retrieved from her other houses.

Above: Reconstruction drawing of the Forest Great Chamber using evidence from the 1601 inventory

Below: *Detail of the plaster frieze in the Forest Great Chamber, which would once have been painted*

4 BUTTERY

The processional route from the Forest Great Chamber to the Hill Great Chamber would have continued overhead, above the route back through the hall. The central corridors in the second and third floors are visible as blocked doorways above the hall. The best bedchamber suite, with a withdrawing room and private closet, was over the hall. The bedchamber with its handsome overmantel can be glimpsed by going through the middle service door in the long wall of the hall into the former buttery.

The buttery was for storing beer (a weak brew, the staple household drink) and next to it was the pantry for storing bread. The buttery and pantry, here contained within the same space, were under the control of the usher, or butler. In a conventional medieval house, with a main doorway into a screens passage at the low-status end of the hall, there would have been three doors along the passage, leading to the buttery, kitchen and pantry. Here the new-style hall does not have a screens passage, so the three doors (one now blocked) are spread along the length of the hall. This is a radical change of layout for a hall, but it still separates the services from the high-status great stairs on the other side of the hall.

The rooms above the buttery were reached from the secondary stairs. The first floor had a servant's room with a storage room called the wardrobe next to it. The wardrobe, the medieval name for a room storing textiles, contained a large cupboard, which has now come to mean a wardrobe as a piece of furniture. The second-floor rooms are visible from the stairs, as is the top-floor bedchamber, although its fine overmantel can only be viewed from here.

5 KITCHEN, 6 LARDER AND 7 PASTRY

The route to the kitchen passes the foot of the sweeping, secondary stairs. To the left of the door is a serving hatch for the cooks to pass out dishes. The kitchen is well preserved, with two open fireplaces for roasting and boiling. The niche on the north wall once contained a water cistern, filled by water channelled through underground pipes. Rooms over the kitchen tended to be warmer, which may explain why the nursery was above it. The kitchen was furnished with four trestle tables. Food was stored in the two larders beyond the lobby outside the south doorway. The upper larder was for dry goods; the lower one was used as a cellar. The door leading out to the service yard opened on to the brewery and storage rooms, where extra cooking dishes and iron spits were kept. The pastry has intact brick-lined ovens, sitting back to back with the kitchen flue. This was the kitchen for baking. It leads back to the rear of the secondary stairs.

These stairs are so impressive, with a leisurely rise to half-landings, that it is wrong to think of them as just for the servants. Their spacious flights are a forerunner of the larger great stairs that Bess created in the New Hall. On the way up, some original timber balustrades survive, as does some Elizabethan plaster flooring.

Below: The great arch of the kitchen fireplace with a brick insert of the late 1700s

Bottom: A reconstruction drawing of the kitchen using evidence from the 1601 inventory

Saving the Plasterwork

Hardwick Old Hall has a very unusual and extensive set of Elizabethan plaster overmantels, as well as important decorative wall plaster in the Forest and Hill Great Chambers. It is remarkable that these features have survived as well as they have in this ruined house, open to the weather. One of the reasons for their survival is because little roofs have been put over each panel to throw rainwater forward. These were first installed during a conservation campaign in 1911. The duke of Devonshire invited the experts at the Society for the Preservation of Ancient Buildings to oversee essential repairs to the house, which was still partially roofed. The repairs were meant to stand out, so that they could not be confused with Elizabethan work. The distinctive tiles used to fill holes are still easy to spot around the house. The first plaster protection roofs were also made of tiles, but they have now been replaced by lead. The plaster, like the stonework, was also heavily blackened by industrial soot, deposited from the region's historic textile, coal and mineral activities.

Routine monitoring of the condition of the plasterwork is a challenge, without floors to walk on; conservators have to use mountaineering ropes. An extensive programme of works took place in 2001, when scaffolding enabled the plasterwork to be cleaned and recoated in limewash. Fragments of untreated plaster are on display in the west lodge.

Below: Detail of the plasterwork from the Forest Great Chamber frieze

8 MR WILLIAM CAVENDISH'S CHAMBER

This first-floor room is called Mr William Cavendish's chamber in the 1601 inventory. William was Bess's second and favourite son, named after her second husband. This was probably the room that William used before he and his wife Ann moved out of the Old Hall to their own house nearby at Owlcotes. The room was originally fitted out from floor to ceiling with oak panelling, which had good insulating properties. It would also have benefited from the heat from the bread ovens in the pastry below. A timber partition separated this room from a smaller room, known as a closet, which was used as a dressing room or study. The elegant strapwork plaster overmantel is visible from the pastry below.

The corridor between this room and the nursery (with its plaster overmantel of a biblical scene from the story of Tobias and the angel) leads out to the brewhouse block and the latrine tower beyond. Other rooms would have had chamber pots, carried away by servants.

9 MR DIGBY AND MR REASON'S CHAMBERS

On the second floor, the two rooms reached through the central corridor are named in 1601 as belonging to Mr Reason and Mr Digby. They were gentlemen servants in Bess's household, who qualified for spacious rooms with elegant fittings. Mr Digby was probably a relative of Bess. In 1601 his room was simply furnished with a bedstead and panelling under the window, which may suggest that it was not in use at the time. In contrast, Mr Reason's room had an elaborate four-poster bed. The corridor continued past more gentlemen's chambers towards Bess's own suite at the east end of the house. There is also a corridor out to the latrine tower on this floor. It runs past two good sets of bedrooms and their closets, fully furnished in 1601 with tapestries, four-poster beds and richly embroidered red bed-hangings.

First floor

Second floor

Left: Mr Reason and Mr Digby's chambers with their fine plaster overmantels

Right: View of the state suite on the third floor, with the withdrawing chamber over the hall, marked by the window to the right of the main gable

🔟 BEST BEDCHAMBER

The third-floor landing on the secondary stairs marks the arrival at the most impressive rooms in the house, although important guests would have walked across to here from the great stairs to the east. We know this because we can see that two doorways open away from the visitor into the correct sequence. From this side, we can only look back through the doorway coming out of the best bedchamber suite, probably into the inner chamber. This room was panelled, and led off to the room with the most lavish overmantel, which is, unfortunately, impossible to see from this position. This is probably part of the main bedchamber suite, which consisted of a withdrawing room, the bedroom and a smaller closet or dressing room.

It is impossible now to be certain which room was which, but it is tempting to link the most expensively upholstered bed, listed in the 1601 inventory, with the powerful heraldic overmantel, as part of a richly furnished interior. The suite was furnished with the finest tapestries, upholstery and furniture in the house. The sumptuous bed was a four-poster, the head and posts of which were gilded and inlaid. It was covered with a velvet canopy and hung with red and yellow silk damask curtains, trimmed with gold and red lace. Both the canopy and the bedhead were embroidered with coats of arms, presumably to match the chimney's overmantel, which is of Bess's coat of arms with her heraldic beasts – the Hardwick stags, adopted by the Cavendish family as their heraldic supporters. The bedspread was made of gold and purple striped satin. The great chair was upholstered in crimson velvet with embroidered motifs in gold. Two Turkish carpets, considered by Elizabethans as too rare to be walked on, were fashionably displayed on a table and a cupboard.

The withdrawing chamber linked to the bedchamber was equally richly furnished and by 1601, it was hung with tapestries. It had an open cupboard for displaying gold and silver tableware, with a Turkish carpet covering the top. Two important armchairs were carved, gilded and upholstered with black striped taffeta, set off with purple cushions, trimmed with gold and silver lace and silver fringing.

This suite was not for Bess, however, as her bedchamber is listed as being on the floor below. This was the state suite, intended for the most important guest and to be seen by all of Bess's honoured guests as they walked from one great chamber to the other, impressed by her taste and wealth. On leaving the Forest Great Chamber at the east end of the house, they passed the head of the great stairs and entered the centre of the house, literally and symbolically occupied by the best bedchamber suite.

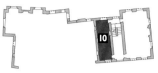

Third floor

Below: Reconstruction drawing of the best bedchamber in the state suite showing the surviving plaster overmantel and furnishings listed in the 1601 inventory

Above: The west and north windows in the Hill Great Chamber with the deep plaster frieze of a double arcade

Facing page above: The massive stone chimney surround with the plaster overmantel, whose giant figures gave the room its later name of the 'Giants' Chamber'

Below: Reconstruction drawing of the Hill Great Chamber based on a drawing made in 1775 for the panelling. The plaster does not seem to have been painted

▥ HILL GREAT CHAMBER

This impressive room would have been the highlight for visitors in Bess's time. By day, light flooded in from the huge windows. The north-facing windows look out towards Bolsover Castle, owned by Bess's son, Sir Charles Cavendish. The windows on the fireplace wall face west, in the direction of Chatsworth, the home Bess created with her husband Sir William Cavendish. The south windows look towards South Wingfield Manor, a property of her last husband, the earl of Shrewsbury, and a temporary home for Bess while she built the Old Hall.

Here family and guests would have dined in state, in this great double-height room, sitting at a long table 'with postes and frame carved', according to the inventory. Two cupboards for displaying rich tableware were covered with Turkish carpets. Otherwise this room was simply furnished, relying on the impact of the windows and the extraordinary plasterwork.

A drawing of the room, made in 1775, shows how strongly the decoration was influenced by Renaissance art (see page 35). The room is also full of design elements taken from Roman architecture. The arches of the wall plaster divide the walls into a double arcade – a feature just becoming fashionable in northern Italian houses. The arcades were complemented by the elegant plaster frieze of fronds of foliage and flowers, centred on grinning masks, which ran round the cornice. The geometric panelling that lined the lower walls was divided into sections by fluted pilasters, or flat columns, in the Ionic style. It is possible that some of these pilasters are now in the New Hall, in Mary, queen of Scots's room, moved there by the sixth duke in the 1850s. The capitals on the pilasters are decorated with three flowers, eglantines or wild roses, which were part of Bess's coat of arms.

The giant plaster figures on the overmantel are dressed as Roman soldiers, but it is not clear who they represent. They may perhaps be Mars and Hercules. These figures gave rise to people calling this room the 'Giants' Chamber', but Bess knew it as the Hill Great Chamber, sitting as it does on the edge of the escarpment.

Third floor

Bess used the design of the central panel of the overmantel to make a point about her long life and steady rise in society. Like most of the decorative plaster panels in the house, the source of inspiration comes from an artist's print, given to the plasterers to copy. We know the name of the master plasterer – Abraham Smith – from the building accounts. The winged figure is copied from a Flemish engraving, published in 1559, that shows the triumph of Patience, sitting on a carriage, over Desire, who is being made to pull the carriage, and over Fortune, who has to follow behind. Like other educated Elizabethans, Bess was familiar with symbols and signs worked into decorative schemes, and would have expected her guests to understand the reference.

If her guests knew anything about their host, they would have known that Bess had outlived four husbands and had overcome debts, legal challenges and political intrigue. She was confidently handing over unthinkable wealth and lands to her sons. Patience had certainly won over life's many setbacks.

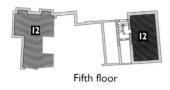

Fifth floor

Below: A detail of the New Hall skyline with its banqueting houses and chimneys

🔢 ROOF WALKS

The secondary stairs continue to rise up to a fifth floor, which would have brought visitors in Bess's time out onto the lead roof over the Hill Great Chamber. At the other end of the house, smaller stairs went up onto the roof over the Forest Great Chamber. Bess's household and her guests could have enjoyed a walk round the perimeter of the roof, safely behind the stone balustrade, taking in the extensive views over the park and the landscape beyond. Other large Elizabethan houses had little rooms perched on their roofs, known as banqueting houses. Here dinner guests could go up to enjoy a dessert course of fruit, nuts and sugar confections. The roofline of the New Hall with its six tower rooms, sparkling with glass, shows how these banqueting houses added to the impact of the architecture.

The Old Hall skyline is still impressive with the one surviving stair tower, but there were no separate banqueting houses on its roof. The 17th-century drawing shows the original impact of the Old Hall roofline, with balustrades around both ends of the house. The two stair towers are accompanied by great slabs of chimney stacks. Elizabethans treated chimneys as decorative features when they could be seen close up by visitors on the lead roof. The chimneys for the New Hall look like classical columns, ornamented with raised panels.

Masons' Marks

Hardwick Old Hall has a number of intriguing marks carved on the smoothly finished stone of doorways, windows and fireplaces. These are masons' marks, made by the stone masons to enable their work to be identified, which was essential when they were paid only for the work done, not by a daily rate.

It is also very helpful to architectural historians interested in following craftsmen between different jobs. Because so much of Elizabethan architecture was designed by the master masons, who led a team of stone masons, their experience and style preferences are important factors in determining the final look of the building. Matching up marks between different buildings allows us to suggest that the same craftsmen worked on all of them, which may explain similarities if we no longer have records of who designed the buildings. It also shows us how far craftsmen travelled between jobs, which is another guide to how valuable and unusual their skills were.

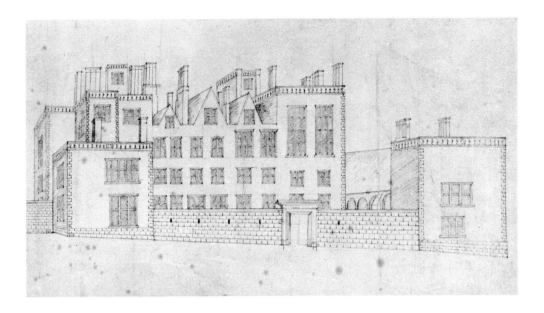

⬛ LODGES AND SERVICE YARD

This drawing, made in the mid-17th century, is an important record for the appearance of the house, although the ground-floor windows are obscured by the forecourt wall and the porch is not shown. The drawing also shows a structure over the present service yard, with an arcade or row of arched windows. This might be the tennis court, documented in 1642 but possibly built earlier.

The two lodges set into each corner of the forecourt were built by Bess's son William. The massive timbers of the west lodge stairs and of the east lodge roof have been dated by dendrochronology to 1625, the likely date for the trees to have been felled. The lodges probably replaced earlier, smaller buildings shown in the 1610 survey plan. The two lodges are similar in plan, with two rooms to each floor and a central staircase, although the west lodge has a lower storey, taking advantage of the steep slope of the hillside.

The lodges were probably originally built to provide extra bedrooms for higher-status servants, as each spacious room is well lit and has a fireplace. They remained in use, although the east lodge was converted into a laundry, before being refitted in 1924 as a cottage, for the use of the night watchman. Each lodge had half of the Old Hall forecourt as its garden.

The west lodge remained as a residence until the 1950s, when it had the advantage of a chicken run and extra storage in the Old Hall's service yard. It was refurbished for use as the visitor reception between 1996 and 1997, which was a good opportunity to analyse the history of its redecoration. Paint samples show how frequently the woodwork was repainted, from dark green to imitation wood grain. The present shop was the kitchen, whose lead sink is still set in to the window sill, now hidden under a flap. The exterior of the east lodge has been plastered in traditional fashion to cover the rough local stone.

Above: This drawing of the north front of the Old Hall and lodges was probably made in the mid-17th century and shows the complex skyline of the house

Below: The conduit house, behind the house, was a distribution point for water for the house, supplying the kitchen cistern

History

Estranged from her husband, Bess returned to Hardwick – her childhood home – in her sixties. She completely rebuilt her father's medieval manor house, creating a fashionable and innovative house, in keeping with her status as countess of Shrewsbury, and celebrating her rise to wealth and power.

Left: Detail of the plaster frieze and tapestries in the High Great Chamber of the New Hall. The chairs were used by Bess's grandson the second earl and his wife

MEDIEVAL HARDWICK

Hardwick is in the parish of Ault Hucknall, known from the Domesday survey. Bess's ancestor Joscelin of Stainsby was given a grant of lands at Hardwick (meaning 'sheep farm') by 1253. Joscelin was a lawyer, who had a chapel in his hall at Hardwick. (The Hardwick family surname emerged by 1340.) The Hardwicks owed their feudal allegiance to the Savage family. The Savage estate was the manor of Stainsby, the large parish of Ault Hucknall and the parish of Heath. Bess ended up purchasing the Savage estates in 1593, in a neat reversal of old family relationships.

The medieval Hardwick family was minor gentry, farming its small estate of about 300 acres. Ten years before Bess's brother James died in 1581, his property was described as the hall with courts, barn yards and dovecote yard, a park, and the farming estate. It earned him £341 a year. We do not know what the house Bess was born in looked like, but it would have been a small manor house with a central hall and perhaps small wings at each end for parlours, bedchambers and the kitchen. James Hardwick refurbished the house but got himself into debt; Bess might have finished it off when she bought back the estate from his creditors after his death. It has been suggested that the only trace of the old house can be seen on the fireplace wall of the present great hall.

Below: The south front showing the external appearance of the great hall's chimney to the right, getting narrower as it rises

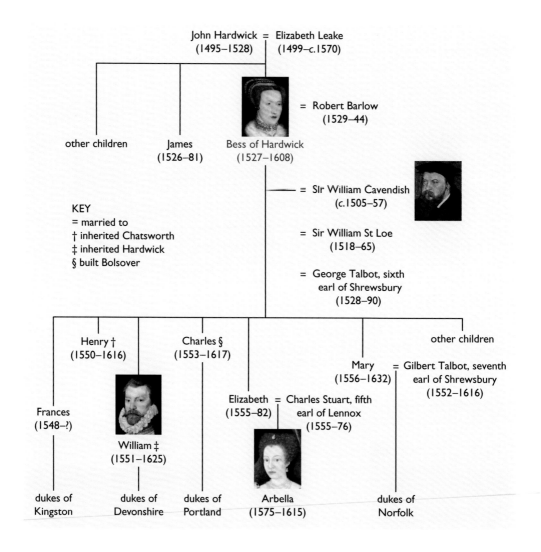

John Hardwick = Elizabeth Leake
(1495–1528)   (1499–c.1570)

other children

James
(1526–81)

Bess of Hardwick
(1527–1608)

= Robert Barlow
(1529–44)

= Sir William Cavendish
(c.1505–57)

= Sir William St Loe
(1518–65)

= George Talbot, sixth
earl of Shrewsbury
(1528–90)

KEY
= married to
† inherited Chatsworth
‡ inherited Hardwick
§ built Bolsover

Henry †
(1550–1616)

Charles §
(1553–1617)

other children

Mary
(1556–1632)

= Gilbert Talbot, seventh
earl of Shrewsbury
(1552–1616)

Frances
(1548–?)

Elizabeth = Charles Stuart, fifth
(1555–82)   earl of Lennox
               (1555–76)

William ‡
(1551–1625)

dukes of
Kingston

dukes of
Devonshire

dukes of
Portland

Arbella
(1575–1615)

dukes of
Norfolk

Above: Bess's family tree showing her ultimate aristocratic descendants

Certainly the masonry at the base of the wall is much altered but it is impossible to say with certainty that Bess went on to build her new house in 1587 around this tiny fragment. If she did choose to rebuild right on top of the site of the old house, this may explain the odd alignments between the east end and the west end of her house. This question can only be answered by archaeological excavations. Some of the surviving timber in the Old Hall has been dated by dendrochronology to about 1500, so it might have come from the old manor house.

BESS OF HARDWICK

Bess was born in 1527 to John Hardwick and Elizabeth Leake. She was one of six children, five girls and one boy, James, who would inherit his father's estate. Bess's family were able to place her in an aristocratic household to receive an education suitable for a gentlewoman. This move away from her home introduced her to powerful social networks centred on the court of Queen Elizabeth I. Bess was married four times. Her first marriage aged 15, to Robert Barlow, took place after she left home at 12 to serve Lady Zouche in her household. They were both children, and the marriage was not consummated. Bess gained her first experience of handling legal proceedings when she went to court to claim her widow's dower. (Robert had died on Christmas Eve 1544, aged 14.) Bess later served Lady Frances Brandon, a princess of royal blood, who was the wife of Henry Grey, marquess of Dorset, and mother of Lady Jane Grey. While in this household, she met Sir William Cavendish, whom she married in 1547, aged 19. Sir William Cavendish was 40, already a widower with three children, and had achieved considerable wealth through his Court connections. Bess was presented at Court and quickly took charge of her husband's estate and household accounts.

In 1549, Bess and Sir William purchased the Derbyshire estate of Chatsworth, once the home of her stepfather Ralph Leche. They began to make this their principal country seat. Sir William negotiated an exchange of his southern lands for new Derbyshire lands from the Crown. To embellish their new property, Sir William commissioned a new house at Chatsworth, and building work began while they lived in the old house. Sir William ended his life a sick man, charged with embezzlement of £6000, dying suddenly while under investigation in 1557.

Left: Portrait of Bess's second husband, Sir William Cavendish, aged 44 (artist unknown)

BUILDING CHATSWORTH

Bess consequently found herself a widow with six young children, three step-daughters and a huge debt, which far outstripped the annual income of £350 or £400 a year from her husband's estates. Sir William had anticipated his death, however, in his financial arrangements. Bess was left the entire estate for her lifetime, and only Chatsworth house and its estate were entailed on their eldest son Henry after her death. When the case to reclaim Sir William's debt finally came to be heard, it was 1563 and Bess had married one of Elizabeth's favoured courtiers, Sir William St Loe. The queen pardoned the debt on payment of a fine of £1000, which her new husband paid on behalf of his wife.

Bess recommenced the building works at Chatsworth, where her mother was living with the Cavendish children. Her new husband, Sir William St Loe, called her 'the chief overseer of my works'. Bess was largely required to reside at Court, as she was appointed one of the ladies of the privy chamber to Elizabeth. This was a great honour, the second of four ranks of court ladies who served the queen.

Sir William St Loe expressed his love for Bess by transferring everything to her through a deed of gift, and by drawing up a will that left everything to her and her heirs forever. Sadly, Sir William died suddenly in February 1565. Bess probably began a series of additions to Chatsworth from this date, including a new top floor of state rooms. The new interiors were being finished after 1576, perhaps for a royal visit.

COUNTESS OF SHREWSBURY

Two years later, George Talbot, sixth earl of Shrewsbury, who was a widower, began to court Bess. He was one of the richest men in the country, with vast landed holdings north of the river Trent. The Talbot family seat was Sheffield Castle. Bess accepted his proposal of marriage, and negotiated the marriage jointure to keep Chatsworth House and some other properties under her direct control. Rents of some Shrewsbury properties were given to her for life. Her son and heir Henry Cavendish married Grace Talbot, and the earl's son and heir Gilbert Talbot married Bess's daughter Mary Cavendish in 1567. This double marriage tied the two families together beyond the lifetimes of their respective parents. Bess married Shrewsbury soon afterwards.

They had just a year to establish their married life before Shrewsbury was appointed the custodian of Mary, queen of Scots, after her forced abdication. Mary Stuart (1542–87) had been deposed by a faction of Scottish nobles. She escaped to England, where the complex religious and dynastic relationship of the Stuarts to Elizabeth resulted in an English policy to keep her imprisoned. (Her infant son, James VI, succeeded her and would go on to unite the English and Scottish crowns as James I.) Shrewsbury's increasingly onerous and expensive task would

Above: Bess's third husband, Sir William St Loe, in full armour
Below: Bess's fourth husband, George Talbot, sixth earl of Shrewsbury

Facing page: Bess of Hardwick as a young woman. She is wearing beautiful fur-lined clothes and jewels, suggestive of her wealth and status

Right: Portrait of Queen Elizabeth I, by the studio of Nicholas Hilliard. Bess served as one of her ladies of the privy chamber

Right: Portrait of Queen Elizabeth I, by the studio of Nicholas Hilliard. Bess served as one of her ladies of the privy chamber

last for 15 years, and required the couple to lock themselves away with Mary, so close was her supervision supposed to be. Bess managed the complex domestic affairs with her usual brilliance, taking on the Scottish royal household in exile and Mary's incessant requirements. She organized the repair and furnishing of Tutbury Castle, Staffordshire, for them all, ancient and damp as it was (the earl leased the Tutbury estate from the Crown). They all managed to travel to warmer residences such as Wingfield Manor or take the spa waters at Buxton occasionally, but only by royal consent. Even Shrewsbury's wealth could not sustain this level of expense; Bess shrewdly bailed him out in return for gifts of land for her Cavendish children.

Bess used the visit of her friend Margaret, countess of Lennox, as the occasion to scheme a marriage for her daughter Elizabeth to Margaret's son Charles Stuart in 1574. Margaret was of royal blood, as the granddaughter of Henry VII, and as a Catholic was considered a threat by the English queen. Her grandson by her other son Henry, Lord Darnley, and Mary, queen of Scots, was the Scottish infant king James VI, a likely heir to the English throne. Bess knew that she should first have asked for permission from the queen. Elizabeth objected to the illicit marriage. She instituted an official investigation and imprisoned Lady Lennox in the Tower of London for three months. Whatever Bess's ambitions were, a baby daughter, Arbella was born – another potential claimant to the English throne.

RETURN TO HARDWICK

In 1581 Bess's brother James Hardwick died a debtor in the Fleet prison, and the Hardwick estate was seized by the lord chancellor's department. Bess was a principal creditor, since she had made loans to James in return for mortgages on property. She bought the estate back from the Crown two years later, for £9,500. The old house became her son William Cavendish's home, while she lived in Chatsworth. By now she was also caring for young Arbella, orphaned in 1582. However, for some time her marriage had been under strain. Shrewsbury was probably suffering from the financial and political long-term strain of serving two queens and may even have suffered a personality-altering stroke. His difficult temper became

Left: Bess's granddaughter, Lady Arbella Stuart aged 13, painted in 1589

Above: Bess's main residences

1 Sheffield Castle

Seat of the Talbot family

2 Buxton

Where Mary, queen of Scots, went to take the spa waters at the earl of Shrewsbury's house

3 Chatsworth House estate

Purchased by Bess and her second husband Sir William Cavendish

4 Hardwick

Where Bess built the Old and New Halls

5 Wingfield Manor

Bess's temporary home, owned by her husband the earl of Shrewsbury

6 Tutbury Castle

Where Bess and the earl of Shrewsbury supervised Mary, queen of Scots's imprisonment

intolerable to Bess and in 1584 she fled Chatsworth under threat of attack from her husband's retainers. By 1587 all attempts at reconciliation, including the personal intervention of the queen, had failed. Bess was still exiled from Chatsworth, and turned her energies to rebuilding at Hardwick.

Shrewsbury died, alone and worn out, in 1590. Bess was now mistress of the lands that she had purchased, those that had come to her through her previous marriages, and to one third of the Shrewsbury estate income, as well as her life interest in some of the Shrewsbury properties. Aged 63, a dowager countess, a longstanding friend of the queen, with a granddaughter, Arbella Stuart, in line for the throne, Bess had the money and the freedom to make firm provision for the future success of her descendants. It was only in the geographical sense that she was back where she had started, at Hardwick.

HARDWICK AS THE NEW CAVENDISH HOME

Bess's first country house project was the courtyard house at Chatsworth. The design was drawn up by a master mason as a ground plan. Work began in the 1550s, and its form echoed the late medieval fortified courtyard house, entered through a great gatehouse. A whole generation later, in the 1580s, the English country house was beginning to take on a very different form. The latest houses were not built around courtyards. They were compact in plan, emphasizing height and making new, more sophisticated, use of the language of classical architecture to define their proportions. Some of the new houses revealed a playful approach to geometry. Using angled walls, projections and recesses, their designers moulded the compact houses into complex plan forms, rendered in three dimensions. Bess embraced these changes when she embarked on her building projects at Hardwick, first at the Old Hall and then with more finesse at the New Hall.

Right: Wollaton Hall by Robert Smythson, which might have influenced Bess at Hardwick

Bess might have been thinking ahead about the estates under her control after her death. Chatsworth was entailed on her son Henry, whom she did not hold in high regard (he had sided with Shrewsbury against her). William was her favourite, studious son and already living in the medieval manor house at Hardwick with his wife and young son. Bess's principal residence away from Court was the Shrewsbury property, South Wingfield Manor, which she was able to occupy by agreement with her irascible husband after the intervention of the queen. Hardwick was the obvious candidate for new investment, combining her own roots with the promise of a fresh start for the Cavendish dynasty, through a son she both controlled and trusted. It was also only seven miles from Wingfield, allowing Bess to visit frequently to supervise progress.

The most popular architect at the time was Robert Smythson (1534/5–1614). He initially worked for patrons in the south, but in 1580 he came to Nottinghamshire to build Wollaton Hall, and never went south again. His distinctive design hand appears in houses in Nottinghamshire, Derbyshire, Staffordshire, Lincolnshire and Yorkshire. Bess would have seen his buildings at first hand from the commissions that the earl of Shrewsbury made at Worksop in the 1580s, shortly after their neighbour Sir Francis Willoughby had used him at Wollaton Hall. She certainly commissioned him to design the New Hall from 1590, but there is no evidence that he helped her with the Old Hall first. Apart from personal experience of the new style of country houses, Bess's presence at Court also put her in a good position to learn about courtiers' building projects, and she received plenty of details about her friends' houses from her correspondents when in the country.

Above: Wingfield Manor, built in about 1435, was Bess's temporary home
Below: Wotton Lodge, Staffordshire, another compact high house designed by Robert Smythson, the architect of the New Hall

Above: The High Great Chamber in the New Hall with the deep plaster frieze showing the goddess Diana, probably intended to be a compliment to Elizabeth I

INNOVATION AT HARDWICK OLD HALL

The form of the Old Hall is notable for the axial great hall, entered centrally and symmetrically positioned in the middle of the house. The house is also unusual in having two great chambers, placed high on the top floor, instead of on the first floor. There was also a central corridor through the second and third floors, another unusual feature for the time.

Bess was one of the first patrons in England to reverse medieval precedent and turn her own great hall through 90 degrees, following the newly fashionable Italian villa design made famous by Andrea Palladio. Sir Christopher Hatton had experimented with this slightly earlier at the banqueting house at Holdenby. Bess was probably also aware of continental architectural books discussing the new fashions. In Palladio's villas, the central hall was no longer able to dominate the principal façade, because its length was buried in the depth of the building. Consequently, the dominant structural features at the Old Hall were the two high great chambers crowning the skyline. These were the principal rooms for the kind of formal entertaining, which was appropriate for a countess and for her royal granddaughter, Arbella. Although the realization of the plan of the Old Hall is a little lopsided, we can see that Bess chose an innovative plan that made symmetry a priority, emphasized by having a great chamber at each end. Placing the hall in the centre of the house and building floors over it would become the dominant design for the English country house until the middle decades of the 18th century.

THE NEW HALL

Even before the rebuilding of the Old Hall was complete, Bess had ordered the construction of foundations for a new house, just metres away, in 1590. This would become the New Hall, the building in which she would refine some of the details of the Old Hall with the help of the architect Robert Smythson. The New Hall has a very strong geometric plan, and the four corner towers emphasize its height. The New Hall also develops the innovative features first seen in the Old Hall: the central great hall, the elegant sweep of the stone stairs and the drama of the forest frieze in the great chamber. This time there is only one great chamber, on the top floor. Bess provided a route from each end of the state rooms, using the long gallery along the length of the house – a feature not seen in the Old Hall.

Both houses continued to be built at the same time; the Old Hall was being finished off in 1596 and Bess was able to move into the New Hall in 1597. In 1592, she started building a new house on a nearby estate for William and his family to live in, at Owlcotes. When he moved out, Hardwick was just for her and Arbella.

The surviving accounts do not show many purchases of furniture, suggesting that the contents of the two halls were taken from Chatsworth. The New Hall has important survivals from Bess's furnishings, the most famous being the embroideries and the French-influenced furniture. Bess excelled at needlework – a pastime suitable for ladies. The inventory made in 1601 of the contents of both halls shows that the Old Hall was richly furnished, but we do not know what happened to the contents before the partial demolition in the 1750s.

Some of the early portraits now in the New Hall might have hung in the Old Hall, which we know had 20 portraits in Bess's lifetime. The expensive sets of tapestries in the Old Hall might have been rehung, as some rooms in the New Hall now contain tapestries that were not there originally. Plain panelling now in the drawing room and the dining room was put there by the sixth duke of Devonshire in the 1840s. This might have been recycled from the Old Hall rooms. There are four framed panels of stained and inlaid wood on the chapel stairs, brought from the Old Hall by the sixth duke. One is dated 1576, so it must originally have come from Chatsworth.

Below: The entrance front of the New Hall. The tallest windows mark the state rooms on the second floor

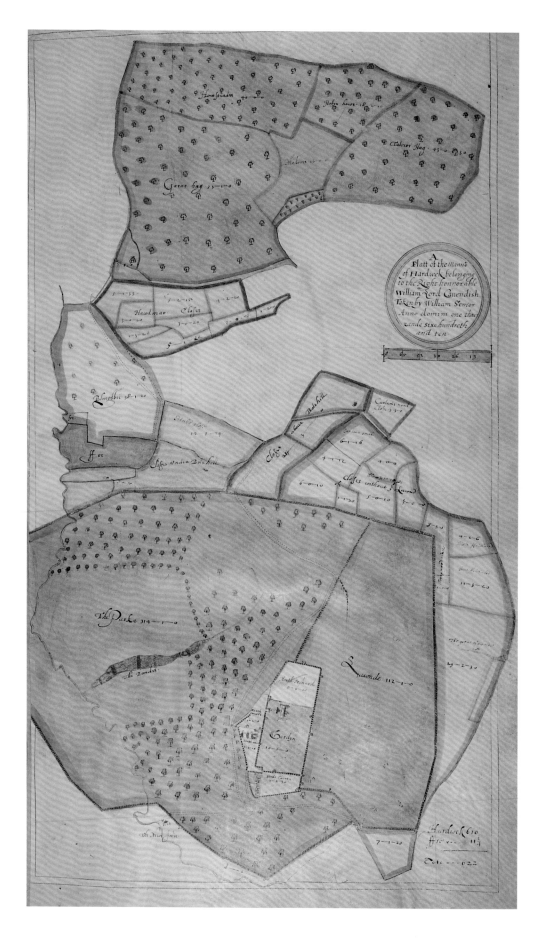

THE CAVENDISH ESTATES

On Bess's death in 1608, her second son William inherited everything, except for the Chatsworth estate, and the smaller estates, which she left to her third son Charles. William, who had become the first baron Cavendish of Hardwick in 1605, commissioned a full survey of his estates, using the professional surveyor William Senior, from 1609 to 1611. The result was an atlas of coloured estate maps with its associated book of surveys, showing a total of 11,500 acres. After Henry Cavendish sold his life interest in Chatsworth to William, and subsequently died in 1616 without legitimate male heirs, the Chatsworth and Hardwick estates were united. Perhaps to reflect the prestige of this landholding and his mother's rank, William gained the rank of first earl of Devonshire in 1618, thanks to Arbella's influence at court. The survey work continued for William's son, the second earl, until 1628. At the end of this lengthy process, the second earl found himself in possession of 97,406 acres, half of which was in Derbyshire, a quarter in Yorkshire and the rest dispersed around nine other counties.

After 1616, there were few major changes made to the estate until the 1700s, when the remodelling of Chatsworth was completed, and the family made it their principal residence. Very little money was spent on Hardwick, although it continued to provide a good income from coal mining at Heath and Hardstoft and from agricultural rents. The first earl also gained smaller amounts from financial investments in voyages to Russia, the East Indies and Virginia, and in the development of the Somers Islands in Bermuda.

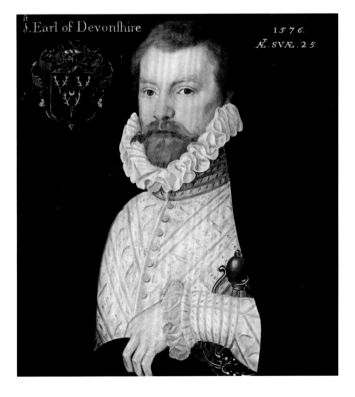

Left: Bess's second son, William Cavendish aged 25 in 1576. He became the first earl of Devonshire in 1618

Facing page: William Senior's 1610 survey map of Hardwick showing the two halls in the larger of two parks

THOMAS HOBBES AT HARDWICK

The philosopher Thomas Hobbes (1588–1679) spent most of
his adult life with the Cavendishes. The first earl appointed the
newly graduated Hobbes as his son William's tutor in 1608.
Hobbes's duties were largely those of a secretary, purse-keeper
and hunting companion, although both young men were
intellectually able. When at Hardwick, Hobbes helped the
surveyor map the estates and also built up a library. Hobbes
and the young William went on an educational tour to
Rome and Venice between 1614 and 1615 and met Italian
intellectuals. Back home, they maintained a friendship with the
philosopher Francis Bacon. Hobbes remained in the Cavendish
household until the untimely death of the young second earl
in 1628. He returned to serve as tutor to the earl's children
in 1630, and developed a friendship with their cousin and
owner of Bolsover, the earl of Newcastle.

Hobbes and the third earl left England for Paris at the
outbreak of the Civil War, to join the Court in exile. Hobbes
returned in 1651, still in the earl's service but free to continue
his philosophical researches. Hardwick accounts show that in
1657 a new library was fitted out for him in the Old Hall, in
the west wing. Hobbes continued to enjoy the patronage of
the family, with summers at Hardwick and winters in London,
enabling him to continue his prolific writings. He died after a
short illness aged 91 at Hardwick and is buried in the parish
church of Ault Hucknall. His reputation as a philosopher of
wide interests, in theology, metaphysics, science, history and
psychology, as well as the political theory he is best known
for, have caused him to be described as 'one of the true
founders of modernity in Western culture'. The Cavendishes
of Hardwick and Bolsover played important roles in supporting
him intellectually, socially and practically. Some of his books,
manuscripts and a library catalogue for Hardwick survive
at Chatsworth.

A PICTURESQUE RUIN

Thomas Hobbes enjoyed the use of the Old Hall as his home, but after his death in 1679, the Cavendishes rebuilt Chatsworth and moved there as their preferred Derbyshire residence. Hardwick was still a valuable estate and the halls were kept in regular repair. But in 1745 the accounts note the demolition of parts of the Old Hall, removing a roof and the tennis court. In 1757 further demolition raised £300 from the sale of lead, iron, plaster, wainscot and doors. This reduced the eastern half of the house to an open shell, but the western side was still roofed and indeed occupied. When the diarist John Byng visited in 1789, the housekeeper and her family were living in the lower rooms, evidenced by the 18th-century bricks in the kitchen hearth and in the fireplace of one of the first-floor chambers. The ceiling of the Hill Great Chamber needed to be supported on props by then, but it remained an intriguing sight for guests to explore. The future Tsar Nicholas I of Russia visited in 1816, apparently finding the state of the Old Hall rather alarming as he climbed the stairs. When Princess Victoria stayed at Chatsworth in 1832, the sixth duke of Devonshire decided the Old Hall was too dangerous for her to enter. The elaborate panelling around the Hill Great Chamber was removed by 1857, and in 1875 ground-floor doorways were walled up, perhaps to keep visitors out and to attempt to stabilize the walls.

The reason for the deliberate dismantling of the Old Hall is not recorded, but it might be an attempt both to economize and create a picturesque garden ruin – a focal point out of the New Hall gardens. The family began to appreciate the Elizabethan halls once again at this time, and the Old Hall's open interior was planted with specimen trees in 1793.

Above: The Hill Great Chamber photographed by Richard Keene in about 1910, still with a floor and a ceiling, which had to be propped up
Below: *Samuel Grimm drew the Hill Great Chamber interior in 1775, showing it as an intact room*

A RUIN RESCUED

In 1908 the ninth duke inherited the title and he tackled the crumbling state of the Old Hall. He commissioned the Society for the Preservation of Ancient Buildings to prepare a plan for repair in 1910. The estimate was for £500 of work, which began in 1911. The society's philosophy was to make modern repairs visible, often using tiles to pack out holes in stonework, as can be seen all around the Old Hall. Like many architectural projects, the final cost was much higher at £2000, but the hall was stable and safe for tourists again.

After the ninth duke died in 1938, his widow, Duchess Evelyn, made the New Hall her home. During the Second World War, from 1939 to 1945, Hardwick park was used as a training camp for airborne soldiers and a camp for Polish refugees. Her son the tenth duke died in 1950, and the 11th duke offered both Hardwick halls and 1000 acres to the government for partial settlement of the death duties payable on his inheritance. This was agreed in 1959, when the estate was transferred to the National Trust and the Ministry of Works took on the guardianship of the Old Hall with a major programme of stabilization work. The smoke-blackened stonework was cleaned in the 1980s; in the 1990s the west lodge was refurbished for visitors and the timber viewing platform built in the Hill Great Chamber. The Old Hall was reopened to visitors, but needs steady care in the face of the sharp Derbyshire weather, a situation Bess would recognize from 400 years ago.

Below: Well-dressed visitors on a day out to Hardwick park are able to visit the Old Hall. This photograph was probably taken before 1911, when repairs would have stripped the ivy from the walls